QED ESSENTIALS

Let's Read

Eat Me, Drink Me!

Katie Woolley

Quarto is the authority on a wide range of topics.
Quarto educates, entertains and enriches the lives of our readers—enthusiasts and lovers of hands-on living.
www.quartoknows.com

Author: Katie Woolley
Series Editor: Joyce Bentley
Editor: Sasha Morton
Consultant: Helen Marron
Designer: Elaine Wilkinson

© 2019 Quarto Publishing plc

First published in 2019 by QED Publishing,
an imprint of The Quarto Group.
The Old Brewery, 6 Blundell Street,
London N7 9BH, United Kingdom.
T (0)20 7700 6700 F (0)20 7700 8066
www.QuartoKnows.com

Manufactured in Shenzhen, China PP072019

9 8 7 6 5 4 3 2 1

Photo Acknowledgments
Shutterstock: front cover Szasz-Fabian Jozsef; back cover and imprint page Alexander Raths; title page, and p12 Robert Kneschke; p3, p16-17 and 20 Bobex-73; p4-5 Monkey Business Images; p6t images72; p6b ENeems; p7 Shestakoff; p8-9 Alexander Raths; p10l FamVeld; p10r and 20 Yanisa C; p11 and 20 Syda Productions; p13 wavebreakmedia; p14t and 20 Pressmaster; p14b and 20 baibaz; p14r ZouZou; p15 Yakobchuk Viacheslav; p17 Monkey Business Images; p18-19 Jack Frog; p21 Olga Sapegina; p23 Segiy Byhunenko (girl); p23 Tupungato (picture)

All rights reserved. No part of this publication may be reproduced, stored in a retrieval system, or transmitted in any form or by any means, electronic, mechanical, photocopying, recording, or otherwise, without the prior permission of the publisher, nor be otherwise circulated in any form of binding or cover other than that in which it is published and without a similar condition being imposed on the subsequent purchaser.

A catalogue record for this book is available from the British Library.

ISBN: 978-0-7112-4422-1

QED ESSENTIALS

Let's Read

Eat Me, Drink Me!

QED

We eat food. Food helps to keep us fit and well.

Food helps us to move, think and grow.

Fruit and vegetables grow in the sun.

They need water to grow too.

Fruit and vegetables help keep us fit and well.

Fresh food can come in lots of colours.

What colours can you see?

The meat and fish we eat comes from animals.

Milk and eggs come from animals too.

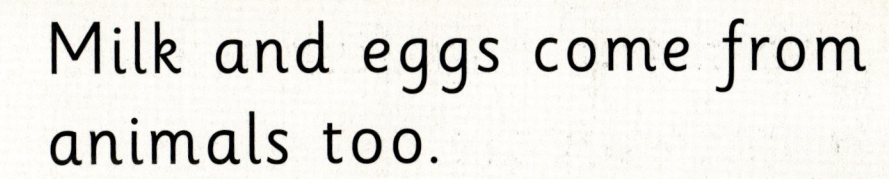

milk

eggs

fish

meat

We need to drink water.

Water helps us move, think and grow.

We eat three meals a day.

breakfast

lunch

dinner

14

What do you like to eat for breakfast, lunch and dinner?

We can eat snacks too.

melon

Fruit and vegetables are good snacks.

Yum!

Cooking is good fun!

Ask a grown-up if you can help cook a meal.

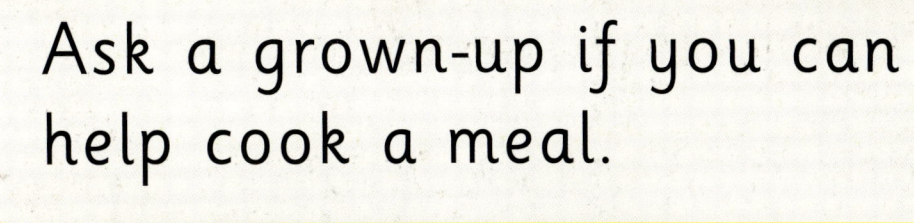

Your Turn

Match it!

Follow the line from each picture to read the word.

lunch

eggs

milk

melon

fish

Clap it!
Say the 'Match it!' words.
Clap and count
the syllables.

Sound it!
Sound out each of these words.

l u n ch   c oo k   g r ow   s n a ck s

Say it!
Read and say these words.

we   play   come   you   are

21

Spot it!

1. Look at page 11. Which word ends with the sound **oo**?
2. Look at page 14. Which word has an **ee** sound?

Finish it!

Look back and find which word is missing.

1. Page 15. What do you _____ to eat for breakfast, lunch and dinner?
2. Page 16. We can eat _____ too.

Count it!

1. Page 12. How many times does the word **to** appear?
2. Page 17. Which word has the most letters?

Answers: **Spot it!** 1 too 2 three **Finish it!** 1 like 2 snacks **Count it!** 1 one 2 vegetables (10 letters)

Sort it!

Sort the letters to spell a word.
Can you find the word in the book?

1. i nk th
2. e r sh f
3. nk d i r
4. l p e h

Do it!

Draw and label a picture of your favourite meal. Yum!

Answers: Sort it! 1 think 2 fresh 3 drink 4 help

23

Notes for Parents and Teachers

Children naturally practise their literacy skills as they discover the world around them. The topics in the **QED Essentials** series help children use these developing skills and broaden their knowledge and vocabulary. Once they have finished reading the text, encourage your child to demonstrate their understanding by having a go at the activities on pages 20–23.

Reading Tips

- Sit next to your child and let them turn the pages themselves.

- Look through the book before you start reading together. Discuss what you can see on the cover first.

- Encourage your child to use a finger to track the text as they read.

- Keep reading and talking sessions short and at a time that works for both of you. Try to make it a relaxing moment to share with your child.

- Prompt your child to use the picture clues to support their reading when they come across unfamiliar words.

- Give lots of praise as your child reads and return to the book as often as you can. Re-reading leads to greater confidence and fluency.

- Remind your child to use their letter sound knowledge to work out new words.

- Use the 'Your Turn' pages to practise reading new words and to encourage your child to talk about the text.

Short, decodable sentences repeat topic words and commonly used words

Wide range of vocabulary to explore in context

Colourful photographs open up further discussion points